BECOMING THE CEO OF YOUR LIFE

Take Control of your Destiny

Napa Bafikele

DISCLAIMER

The author does not accept any liability in the event of any type of loss or damage which may be incurred, directly or indirectly, as a consequence of the application of any content contained in this book.

"When I was a child, I talked like a child, I thought like a child, I reasoned like a child. When I became a man, I put the ways of childhood behind me" (NIV)

1 Corinthians 13:11

DEDICATION

2015 was a year that turned me into a man, I faced my hardest battles physically, mentally, and emotionally. I was at a spaghetti junction of emotions, feeling perplexed and lost. Desmond Taylor stepped up to the plate and helped me in a way I will forever be grateful for. Therefore, I would like to dedicate this book to a great man – Desmond Taylor.

ACKNOWLEDGEMENTS

I would like to thank everyone that purchased this book. Special thanks go to all my family, friends, and acquittances that supported me throughout the journey of writing and publishing this book. Above all, thank you, the readers.

FORWARD

When Napa asked me to contribute to his third book. I was honoured but not totally surprised. Like Napa, I realized I had the ability to direct what happened in each of my 24 hours. Yes, I have a job with a boss/manager. But I am the orchestrator of my life. Ok, we may have to be at work at a set time. But we control what we eat, who we interact with, what we consume and how we spend most of our time. Life is about choices. If you don't make your own, someone else will make them for you. When you start to make your own decisions, you gain a new title. A CEO.

The abbreviation is thrown around a lot, but what does it really mean? Chief Executive Officer, otherwise known as "CEO." The definition states that a CEO is the highest-ranking individual in a company. Responsible for making all major decisions in the direction that the company goes. Everything starts and stops with this one person. Once you've finished this book. You will be that person. But what at which company?

This may sound odd. But think of your life as a company for a second. Think of the people in your life as either customers, employees, or potential clients. You are the CEO. responsible for everything that happens within it. " Good, bad, or indifferent. Wouldn't you want people within your business (your life) to feel content and happy? Wouldn't you want people to be grateful they chose to be in a world that you created? Wouldn't you want the best run company in the world? In case you're wondering, yes should be your answer! So how do you achieve this? Firstly, you keep turning these pages and absorb what Napa has written. All it takes is a choice and a commitment to yourself.

Every company in the world has one. No matter the size, every single one has a CEO. The ones that instantly come to mind, might be Jeff Bezos, Jay- Z or Karen Brady. Now if I asked you to describe them in one word, what would you say? Having Authority? Controlling? Rich or not? If you asked me, I'd say unafraid.

Make no mistake. They aren't any different from you and me. They sleep, eat and breath just the same as we do. The only difference is, they made a choice to take control of their lives and become something great. Unafraid of the pitfalls that have faced so many other businessmen and business-women. Unafraid of the unknown. They only saw the opportunity that taking control of their own lives could bring. There's no reason why you can't do the same!

The first step along that journey was you purchasing this book. So, congratulations are in order. It's important to recognise milestones. Starting something and even thinking about change is an achievement and something to be applauded. So, along this new path you've set out on, don't forget to look back on how far you've come. Now it's time to lay the foundations that will take your life to the next level.

Enjoy the journey. It won't be easy and sometimes old habits take time to shake. But you can't reach new levels doing the same old things you used to. Embrace the new world you are about to enter. You'll thank yourself soon enough.

Jamal Fyfield

Professional Footballer/ Life Coach.

BECOMING THE CEO OF YOUR LIFE.

CONTENTS

DISCLAIMER 3

DEDICATION... 5

ACKNOWLEDGEMENTS.. 6

FORWARD 7

INTRODUCTION 13

CHAPTER 1.
LABELS **16**

CHAPTER 2.
THE DREAM.. **28**

CHAPTER 3.
ROLES AND RESPONSIBILITIES **35**

CHAPTER 4.
MINDSET.. **38**

CHAPTER 5.
THE VISION **50**

CHAPTER 6.
ACTION **56**

CHAPTER 7.
EXECUTIVE POSITIONS **69**

CHAPTER 8.
SKILLS **88**

CHAPTER 9.
MENTORSHIP... **96**

CHAPTER 10.
REFLECTIONS...**104**

FINAL CHALLENGE 107

CONTACT US...108

INTRODUCTION

This book was written over the period of a year. It encapsulates some valuable lessons I have learnt, some mistakes I have made, and my journey to overcome them. The book represents the blueprint that I used to become the CEO of my life. The four pillars of my existence, such as finance, relationships, spiritual and health, improved drastically.

I hope reading my words will bring you inspiration and empowerment via my story and insights into creating a successful individual.

If you are stuck or feel as if you could be more, then this book is written for you. It provides practical tips and useful challenges designed to motivate you to think and change your mindset. It explains the skillset you need to be successful in today's world.

I was inspired to write this book to help anyone who has drifted away from their dreams. It is just a reminder that you can still achieve your dreams regardless of where you are right now. Whether you are broke, uneducated, or even homeless, In the words of the great American motivator, Les Brown, 'It is possible!'

Throughout the book I will offer several tips that will help to keep you on the path towards dream realisation. You will also see the symbol **, which means you may need to stop and reflect on some-thing that was just said or carry out some action.

This is not just another book you read and forget about. This is a self-help companion to foster great-er self-growth, self-discovery, and self-awareness.

CHAPTER ONE

LABELS

"It ain't what they call you, it's what you answer to."
- W.C. Fields

My name is Napa Bafikele.

You may think that sentence is redundant or unnecessary, but I would strongly disagree. I once read somewhere that your name is possibly the only thing that you totally own, yet everybody else uses it more than you. Don't you find that strange?

It's almost ridiculous when you stop to thinking about it. Now that I have mentioned it, you will always remember and think about it. After reading this chapter, you will become more focused when you hear your name, because your name represents more than just another word. It will be so much more than you ever imagined. And once you discover the power that goes with your name, it will never sound or feel the same.

When your name is called, you must learn to listen intently with a heightened sense of discernment. Listen to the voice intonation, see the facial expressions and feel the vibes or energy being emitted. How others address you can reveal a lot about how they feel about you and the value they place on you, though this is often overlooked.

To be honest with you, I only discovered this recently when I encountered some adversity and needed to remind myself of my identity. I needed to tell myself that I am not who others say I am; I am who I am or who I choose to be. I discovered that thinking about this and speaking it aloud had a different impact on my mood, my resilience and my hunger to become a successful entrepreneur.

Therefore, it should come as no surprise that now I regularly remind myself out loud, though mainly in the safety and privacy of my home, that I am Napa Bafikele.

The first time I said my name aloud, it sounded more like a whisper, as if I had no right to call my own name unless I was asked for it; it was strange, even though it had been my name for as long as I could remember. It sounded strange because I had never called my name before reciting it for some nondescript or mundane purpose that required no conscious thought or deeper level thinking. It was like calling a simple word such as 'the' or 'a'. I had written it many times and responded to the person who spoke my name, but I had never called out my own name.

I don't just call my name because I like the sound of it or perform some weird ritual. I call out my name because I have developed an awareness through-out my journey, and now my name represents dif-ferent things.

As a child, it was just a tag or a label that was assigned to me without my input, and when it was spoken, I learnt that there was an expectation and I needed to respond or react. My mother would say 'Napa sit down!' and I would sit down. My teacher would say 'Napa do this task!' and I would do it. No questions asked. My football coach would say Napa you're in the starting line-up and I would do as instructed. As a child, I also recognized the different tonalities that would signify different outcomes when my name was called. A skill that is lost over time. Even at that young age, I could discern through the timbre of the voice whether I was being rewarded or chastised. Let's not forget the dreaded full name call out, which we all know means you're in big trouble.

"Napa Givens Bafikele!"

As I grew older, my name and its meaning started to evolve, and instead of being just a label, it became more. As my character and personality developed, my name started to evoke certain reactions and emotions from those who heard it. It was no longer a tag, it meant more. As a child in school, when my friends heard my name at break time, they smiled. They did not smile because of the simple four-letter word "Napa", but because of the image they attached to it. Napa to them meant 'footballer, comedian and friend'. To some of my teachers, the same simple four-letter word meant trouble, and their facial expressions changed when it was called. My name was changing as I changed, but it was hardly noticeable, even to myself.

When I became a teenager, I became a bit of a lady's man and it would fill me with joy when ladies would smile when they heard my name. I cannot say what emotion or imagery was attached to my name, but it felt good. Without being taught, I somehow learnt to decide my next move depending on how my name was called.

At university, I added something to my name that meant potential employers would now add another layer of value to my name. It was not just Napa Bafikele. It is now Napa Bafikele BSc., MSc. Those six letters earned me a lot of credibility and notoriety. When it was attached to my name, it meant I was in the top ten percent of educated people, which changed the imagery and stereotype that might have been associated with my name.

Later, in my life, I had some personal challenges and my father used words and my name in the same sentences. It made me realise that my name was not just a word. It's a representation of me. The words that were attached to my name caused me to recoil and suffer deep emotional and psychological scars that are still healing. Coming from an African culture, the reality and power of using and saying your name out loud became even more apparent to me. My father's use of my name left me feeling fearful and hopeless at times. I naively believed what he said was true.

Later as I grew into my own strength to recreate my own representation associated with my name, I felt more reassured and my self-esteem, self-belief, and ambition grew. I had to clear my head of other people's beliefs about me and what they associated my name with. I had to develop the right mindset, by standing in front of a mirror and making my positive affirmations. I had to remind my-self that I am Napa Bafikele and tell myself what my name means.

'Other people's opinion should not be your reality'
~ Les Brown.

I am now in control of all aspects of my life. I immersed myself in development to ensure that I was balanced mentally, physically, and spiritual-ly. Because I am Napa Bafikele, I created multiple streams of income to live the life I wanted. Above all, I did not want my fate to be at the mercy of an-other human being.

1st CHALLENGE

Now let me put you to task on some of my skills. Are you ready?

Find a quiet place and sit alone for a minimum of fifteen minutes. Think of the person you would like to become. Be specific in your thoughts. Do not just say I want to be rich and live in a mansion. That means nothing when you stop to think about it in reality.

Why?

Let's imagine you live in a two-bedroom flat in the ghetto and all you have is 87p to your name. I know this sounds like a dismal life and one that you would love to escape. Now imagine that there are millions of people who are homeless, living with fear of death every day and who have not eaten for weeks; to them, you are already rich and live in a mansion.

I believe that many people do not get to their goals because of the lack of specificity in their dreams. The Universe may think it has already given you your request even though it has not been manifested in your life based on your perception. The future is relative.

If you want to be rich, how much money would that be? Do not say ten million and stop there, because ten million Congolese Franc might work out once again at 87p. Get even more specific. Is the money in stock, property, or raw cash in the bank?

I am sure you have watched movies where people discover fairies or genies who promise them their wildest desires. They are then granted their wishes, only to find out that they were not specific enough and lost everything.

One of my favourite recollections was a man aged about sixty who was married to a woman of a similar age. He was given one wish from a genie. He thought long and hard then finally wished that he had a wife who was thirty years younger than him. The genie smiled and thundered 'Your wish is my command. It will be granted when you awake tomorrow!'

That morning, the old man hastened so fast out of bed that he almost broke his hip. With no real thought as to what his wish would be like, he proceeded to search for his bride, only to catch a reflection of himself. His shock and dismay then hit him, "Be careful what you wish for." The genie had aged him by 30 years, making his wife 30 years younger.

When I think about my dream car, the Range Rover Sport. I even see the logo; I know the personalised number plate and colour. I can hear the engine, feel the leather interior. I am in the car. I see myself as I am now because I want it now. On multiple occasions, I have visited the Range Rover dealership just to test drive that car. I went online to build the interior from scratch.

Once you have created the image of the person you would like to become it is now time to add titles and positions to your name. As this book is titled becoming the CEO of your life, let us start with that title. How would you expect to be treated if you were a CEO? Would you rather tell people how to treat you or accept how they decide to treat you?

Remarkably, most people do not tell people how they should be treated. This is especially so in relationships where we become accepting and complacent with the treatment meted out to us by our partners and hide it under the word compromise. This usually leads to the inevitable breakdown of relationships in the long term. Little things that you allow to slip in the name of 'love' will later become an irritant or an annoying habit that drives you crazy.

This will sound harsh, but after you think about it, you will realise it is actually true.

Once you have determined who you are and how you expect to be treated, you need to maintain this in all aspects of your life. It is not enough to create the label, launch a massive promotional campaign, and not deliver. You may never recover your credibility and you will become marked for life.

In 1992, PepsiCo tried to rebrand with a new product, the caffeine-free Crystal Pepsi. It was the new game changer in the drink market, and they tried to sell it as a healthy alternative to their rivals. They went on a massive promotional drive to advertise that they had the newest trendiest drink on the market. The budget was in excess of US $40 million. Coca-Cola naturally stepped up their game too, and entered the market with a new drink to compete.

Initially, the product did well, but most people purchased it out of curiosity rather than being convinced. In the end, the product failed miserably.

You must ensure you have the correct substance to back up your label. We all come across someone we think to be intelligent, driven or friendly, only to be disappointed when we actually meet them in reality. Do not be that person!

Live your brand.

This includes dressing a certain way, walking with the right people, and most importantly, delivering on your word. Integrity is not a lost value. It has withstood the test of time and people trust people who can keep their word. I had a close family friend who was inseparable, like we were joined at the hip. He wanted to start a business within the hospitality sector. I was very excited for him as I always encourage people to become self-independent and explore entrepreneurship. Since the business was at an infant stage and needed capital investment, my friend presented me with the opportunity. During our meeting, we came to an agreement and constructed a contract. For the first six months of the agreement, everything went accordingly. However, in the seventh month, when I was supposed to be getting a larger profit share from the business, my friend wanted to terminate the agreement without a rational reason. The predicament strained our personal relationship and taught me a valid lesson. Because not everyone has integrity when it comes to business, ensure you vet anyone you embark on a business venture with. Most importantly, integrity must be your core value and you deliver on that.

When I entered the property industry, it was my first ever time doing business in a formal manner. Prior to that, I only hustled here and there, nothing very concrete. I did not have to care so much about my brand or what I was doing as long as I was not doing anything illegal.

In the past, when I envisioned a businessman, I would see a man in a suit and holding a briefcase, no facial hair, and a nice haircut. He was also of a completely different ethnicity to mine. This perception made the dream I had seem impossible as I did not feel comfortable with my perceived image.

As if the universe answered my question, I stumbled across two different articles in two days that gave me the confidence to change my mental image. The first article showed a poor woman in tattered clothes talking about some disaster that had affected her family recently. She did not once say she was poor, but her body language and mannerisms told you she was poor financially, mentally and spiritually. She had accepted her life and hope seem like a distant memory.

The second article was of Kim Kardashian wearing ripped up jeans and a ripped t-shirt. It was the same ripped clothes in both articles, but of course, with Kim Kardashian, it was a must-have look. Why? She stepped out in confidence, comfortable with who she was, and told people she was the CEO of her life.

Stepping into Property Investments, I embraced the way I dressed. I am a **VERY** casual guy, and you would be lucky to catch me wearing a suit or shirt. To my surprise, in 2021, when the covid restriction was eased, a friend of mine, Guycha Muele, was getting married. To my surprise, he was looking at my wardrobe. I did not even own a suit. 24 hours prior to the wedding, I had to do an emergency shopping trip to ensure that I looked presentable. The founder of the No Limit record label, who is worth more than 300 million dollars, said something I found very fascinating: "I'm a boss but a suit and tie isn't me." The lyrics still reside with me today.

I also thought that I had to change the way I talk. All of those changes were difficult to come by as I was not being myself. I had long hair when I began my property journey. I remember one man that I highly looked up to telling me that if you ever get a dreadlock or grow your hair even longer, forget business. Immediately, I went to cut my hair, thinking it was a bad decision on my part. You are uniquely you. There are no replicas, only one copy. Being you helps you to stand out and distinguish yourself from the crowd.

With the years I have spent doing business, I have come to quickly realise that people are attracted to you, the person. Now when I get approached on social media or in person, I know who to turn to. People always express the way I carry myself and stay true to my identity. But before you embark on this journey, you first need to know who you are and what you represent.

CHAPTER 2

THE DREAM

"No matter where you're from, your dreams are valid."
— Lupita Nyong'o

From an early age, I had big dreams and a strong desire for the good things in life. I know almost everyone can identify with this as a child, but mine was more than a childhood dream; it became a passion. Instead of fading with age as most childhood dreams do, mine became even more intense as I grew up. I would daydream daily about owning properties and travelling the world.

My dream was inspired by my grandad, who owned properties in the DR. Congo and commanded a level of respect I admired. I would watch him with intense fascination and try to impress him whenever we were in the same space. He was my father figure during my formative years as my dad had migrated to Europe to create a better life for the family.

During those years, having a dad in Europe meant I had everything I physically needed or wanted; it was only years later that I realised it affected me emotionally and psychologically. To date, we do not have a strong bond. For years, the discord lay buried inside me. I did not speak about it to anyone or openly share my feelings. I wanted to maintain a tough, manly exterior for the world to see.

However, a few years ago, I decided to start talking about my journey and my emotions. The first time was extremely difficult as it brought back some very painful memories that I had put in the far recesses of my mind. I am not too proud to admit, I cried. The talking was therapeutic and started me on a journey towards self-healing and inner peace.

Now this might seem completely unrelated to 'Becoming the CEO of Your Life', but it is. One of the things you must come to understand first is yourself, as I explained in Chapter 1.

Who you are is the summation of your background, culture and experiences? Of course, you can change the present, but you must first understand what you are changing about yourself and why.

After I faced my past, I noticed that my outlook and attitude towards life slowly started to change. There were no major changes, just small things. The way I responded to situations. My friends would tell you that in the past, I would not shy away from any confrontation. In fact, I would go looking for confrontations. As I slowly started to unravel my past, I became a calmer person. I responded after thinking through situations. I control my emotions, which permits me to make adequate judgments in situations that may arise. The key thing here is that I learned to be a thermostat, not the thermometer.

I'm slowly becoming more present in my now! I have learned to forgive and accept the things I cannot change. I have also learned to forgive myself. I can never be responsible for another person's actions; I can only control my reactions to them.

One of my favourite prayers is the serenity prayer.

God grant me the serenity to accept the things, I cannot change. courage to change the things I can. and the wisdom to know the difference.

Sometimes we waste so much energy trying to change circumstances and people that it frustrates us and detracts from the vision. Yes, people and circumstances may change, but the wisdom is in knowing the difference.

If there are unresolved issues with people close to you, how does that impact you? It is important to resolve these issues by speaking to a professional to clear your mind and create space for your creativity and success.

"A man's mind may be likened to a garden, which may be intelligently cultivated or allowed to run wild; but whether cultivated or neglected, it must, and will, bring forth. If no useful seeds are put into it, then an abundance of useless weed seeds will fall therein and they will continue to produce their kind."~ **James Allen, As a Man Thinketh**

If you have seeds of anger and distrust and regrets planted in your mind, it will most certainly influence your output. Take the time to create a clear mind so that you can focus on you and your dreams. Here is a quick challenge to recognise the value of this message.

** 2ND CHALLENGE **

Get a piece of paper and write down the word 'CLEAR' in the centre.

Did you do it?

Honestly?

You did not, did you? Humour me and do it. Remember, integrity is doing what you say you will do, even if no one is watching.

Well, if you did, I am guessing you used a clean sheet of paper, right? Why did you do that? You used a clean piece of paper because you could see what you wrote clearly. They were no marks anywhere to distract or confuse what you had written. You did not need to overthink or choose a clean piece of paper, you automatically did. The parts of our life that are controlled by our body and done without our conscious thoughts tend to follow the best-case scenario. We blink without thinking and it works perfectly every time. We need to take lessons from the design of the human machine.

We choose to write on paper that is clean. This also works for our minds. We need to make sure our minds are clear of the things that blur our goals and block our vision. Before you start on your journey, have a mental clear-out. Speak to a self-discovery coach. Forgive and forget and start on a fresh page ready for new ideas to take you to the next level.

A few years ago, I caught up with some friends and invariably the conversation drifted back to our childhood dreams. Every time we gathered as kids, we would boast about our future and all that we would accomplish. As we grew older, the dreams got more elaborate and more specific, up until about the start of secondary school. Up until this point, our dreams were not limited by obstacles or any 'what ifs!' Nothing was impossible. Once we entered secondary school, however, the cracks started to appear. It was here we learnt words like "failure", "grades", and were given career advice based on the data of a child. It was only as an adult that I realised we learn more about life outside of school than within.

Years ago, I heard a story about a child who wanted to climb a great big oak tree. The child next to him told him he was too small to climb that big tree. A lady passing by shouted that he was certain to fall and break his neck. Nevertheless, the young boy started climbing. By this time, a crowd had gathered, and as he looked down, he saw a group of people on the ground shouting and waving their hands in the air.

The young boy smiled and kept going. He eventually got to the top, sat for a while to take in the view, and then came back down. His father pushed through the crowd to embrace him tightly. He then started to talk to the child in sign language. "Why did you climb that big tree?' the dad asked.

'Because everyone was cheering me on,' the boy replied.

It transpired that the boy was deaf, and he mistakenly thought the group was cheering him on to the top. He could not hear their negativity.

TIP #1: Be selective about who you allow to whisper in your ear. Surround yourself with positive people who will support and cheer you to the top.

Over the years, only one thing has changed regarding my childhood dream. My dreams now have definition and specifics, I have also created a pathway to my dream, and I am busy working towards achieving that childhood dream.

TIP #2: Nurture the inner child within you. The one where nothing is impossible, and barriers do not exist. Feed this inner child through imagination and dreams.

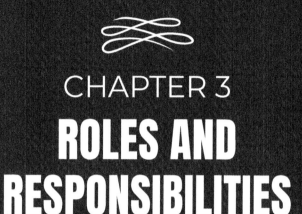

CHAPTER 3
ROLES AND RESPONSIBILITIES

*The man who complains about the way
the ball bounces is likely the one who
dropped it.*
- Lou Holtz

A Chief Executive Officer (CEO) is the most powerful position in any successful company. Although governed by boards of directors with different specialities, the CEO is recognised as the head of the organisation and ultimately makes all the final decisions that can propel the company forward. The CEO is forward thinking, innovative, has a strong work ethic and has a clear vision of the future.

It is not by accident why the leader in any organisation is referred to as the 'head'. The head of the body is instrumental in the logical and rational thought processes and ultimately makes the decisions or choices. Nowhere in history is the top of an executive body referred to as the heart of the hand or the stomach. The head is so named for good reasons.

Are you a CEO?

Do you have the talent and drive to become a CEO?

Though the journey may seem insurmountable, one should focus on the unlimited benefits of being the CEO instead of the obstacles. The freedom to utilise your time as you choose is perhaps the biggest incentive for becoming a CEO.

Imagine getting out of bed not because you have to, but because you choose to. Allocating time towards your success instead of building someone else's dreams?

In addition to time, there is the financial freedom and the peace of mind it brings. Think of the countless material possessions to make life's journey more enjoyable. Yes, I said it. Material possessions to make life's journey more enjoyable. In my experiences the average person somehow feels uncomfortable or even guilty about wanting nice things. Why? Don't you deserve it? Are you less than another human being? From a Christian perspective, some of the greatest millionaires are found in the bible.

The CEO also gets the opportunity to give back to humanity and impact the world in a positive manner. You get to be in a position that can effect change and make this world a better place.

But what does it take to become the CEO of your life? This book will help you chart that journey.

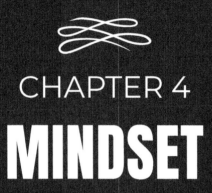

CHAPTER 4

MINDSET

"Once your mindset changes, everything on the outside will change along with it."
- Steve Maraboli

Everything ... begins in the mind of a human.

From the simplest thoughts to life-changing ideas. There are no restrictions or limits to the mind, so we can dream even the most impossible dreams. I imagine at the time the Wright Brothers dreamt of flying that they were ridiculed because it must have seemed impossible to the world. When Marconi told the scientific community about wireless communications, he was mocked and locked in a mental asylum. Yet today, both dreams are part of the reality landscape and are totally accepted within the realms of possibility.

A wise lesson to learn quite early in your journey is that your dreams cannot be seen by anyone else. You can describe the vision, but it will never be the same as seeing the vision yourself. Don't be deterred when people put you down or tell you that your idea will fail and encourage you to change direction. They are not always trying to be mean; they are simply working within the parameters of their experience and knowledge. They may just be projecting their fear of failure onto you.

Remember that two people can look at the same image and see completely different versions, and both will be correct in their interpretation. The difference? mentally your mindset will determine your perspective. Your perspective will determine if you see the glass as half empty or half full. Your ability to see clearly will help you to achieve your vision.

I would like you to take a moment and picture a clock face when it comes to mindset. Imagine, instead of numbers one to twelve written on the clock face, there are words**.** Starting at the top and going in a clockwise direction are the words default, awareness, understanding, identity, vision, passion, resilience, patience, drive, focus, determination and success.

Most people start life on their default factory settings, which basically means they are set according to their parents' background, culture, and beliefs. Think about it and consider some of your parents' mannerisms and beliefs that you now hold, whether religious, political or ritualistic. Most people have never even question why they do certain things in a specific way. They just live each day as it comes.

I once heard an old folklore about a girl from a rural village who grew up watching her mother cook Sunday dinner for the family. Her mother would cut the roast into two parts before putting it in their small oven. The roast was delicious, and everyone loved it. Year after year, her mom would always follow the same ritual. Eventually, the young girl grew up and started her own family in the city. One day, her parents decide to pay her a weekend visit. On Sunday afternoon, the mother and daughter gathered in the kitchen to prepare the Sunday roast.

As the mother sat watching the daughter cook, she observed that the daughter cut the roast in half just as she had done all these years ago, then placed each half in a tin and put it in her large oven. Curious as to why she did that, the mother asked her why she cut the roast in two before baking. "Oh!" she smiled. That's how you cooked all your roasts when I was growing up, 'she replied.

The mother chuckled softly then gently responded 'My child. I only cut my roast in two because my oven is too small. You have an oven that is large enough to fit the entire roast.

The lesson here is that we all do and say things because of those default settings without any conscious thought, sometimes to our own detriment and stalled progress. The limitations your parents had may no longer be relevant to your circumstances. You need to mentally clear your mind before you can chase your dreams. You need to move past twelve o'clock in your life.

3rd CHALLENGE

Choose a day and make a conscious effort to observe the things you do, how you respond and what you think about. Do they all make rational sense? Is the route you take to work the most efficient? Do you wait until the petrol gauge is on E before you refill? How many hours do you spend chatting about nothing? Reflect and re-evaluate! Start your clock moving towards awareness, then slowly develop your identity until you achieve success.

Inevitably, our clock will stop working for some reason. We will all arrive at a crossroads in our lives where we may need to reprogram our mind settings. It could be in our personal or professional lives.

In my short journey, I have been faced with many crossroads and the decisions I have made have steered my life in so many unexpected directions. I may not always have made the right choices, but each choice provided a lesson and helped to create the man I have become.

As I am writing this book and reflecting on my choices, I have realised that there is an increasing maturity in making my decisions. In my early years, my decisions were rash and sometimes ill-informed. But even though it may have led me down painful paths, I still learned a lot of lessons in the process.

I was born in the Democratic Republic of Congo into the Roman Catholic faith. Like many people of African descent, religion formed an integral part of my early life. I would attend church almost every Sunday with my family and take part in all the rites and rituals. I did not understand or question anything, I just accepted that this was the way.

In 2002, I migrated to the United Kingdom and involuntarily embarked on a spiritual transformational journey. I had always attended the church chosen for me with little effort or mental participation. I was literally and figuratively just being dragged along.

This changed when I was seventeen years old and started conversing with other like-minded individuals of the Christian faith. I found myself drawn to their outlook and the principles of their church. I then made a conscious decision to change my denomination and started to worship at Christ In the World Church. To date, this has been one of my biggest mindset changes: deciding which spiritual entity I should worship and how I could do it. Before long, I realised that I felt more connected to my spiritual side and that the mode of worship was more suited for me. I understood the principles and, most importantly, I felt as if I was making a conscious decision instead of being led. Without knowing it then, I had made the first step towards self-awareness and reprogramming my own mindset.

I threw myself into worship and tried to follow all the commandments as closely as possible except one. "*Thou shalt not fornicate.*" As the book is not about my religious journey, I will stop there. It was more satisfying when I decided to follow my own spiritual path instead of the one instilled in me by my parents. It provided mental clarity and it opened my mind to new things.

I have also changed my default settings in my professional life as well. I grew up believing that success could only be guaranteed by a university degree. The more degrees you have, the more likely you are to be successful and change your life and the world. Everyone has heard the rumour that African parents always want their children to be doctors, lawyers or engineers. That was the main drive behind my determination to go as high as possible on my educational journey. At present, I hold a master's degree in Physical Activity, Nutrition, and Health Promotion and although it is not helping me in my current line of work, it still plays a part in my personal life.

An interesting side fact to note: the most educated head of state is the former president of Zimbabwe, Robert Mugabe. A subtle reminder that education can make your journey to the top easier, but it does not guarantee integrity and character.

A good friend of mine spent seven years at university studying architecture, but today he is doing something totally different. The main reason he attended university was because his parents told him to go.

I decided to chart my own path as soon as I realised I was following a pre-chartered course with no personal input. I was merely acquiring degrees based on my family's belief that this was the only way of moving forward and gaining success. After graduating from university, I spent many months working in the health and fitness field. The pay was okay, but I never felt as if I truly belonged there. I could not see myself working in the field until retirement. The confines of four walls and the set salary and set office hours severely impacted my free spirit and love of travel.

I can recall working at a recruitment agency in an effort to expand my horizon and get some flexibility with my time while I try to figure out my own path. The CEO of the company would only come in for a few minutes each day to give instructions and then leave. He drove a black Bentley Continental GT with a private plate of his 2 letter initials. I would always know when he arrived based on the sound of his car engine. It is the same sound I hear when I visualise my dream car. As soon as he entered the office, I would go and stare at his car and daydream, taking in all the fine details. I would study his aura, posture, language and the way he treated his staff. This man was a multi-millionaire and I wanted to be like him and more.

*' The mind is just like a muscle; the more you exercise it, the stronger it gets and the more it expands' ~ **Idowu K***

The journey to create the right mindset will never be smooth. You will face difficulties that will push you back towards your default settings. Only the strong willed will push past this test to create the mindset of a CEO. I think sometimes life tests our resilience to see if we are worthy for the next level. The fundamental skills required in level one of any game will not help you survive level two. It is the same thing with life. Tests come to separate those who can make it to the next level.

For many people, when faced with challenges and failures, they opt to bury their heads, run or play the victim of circumstance card. For others, it is a lesson learnt and the inspiration to push harder and overcome.

I developed my mindset over many years, over many challenges and over many failures.

I remember mentoring two of my clients who were brothers. They identified two rent to rent property deals in Southampton. However, the deal took 6 weeks to negotiate due to unforeseen difficulties in agreeing on the set terms within the final contract. During this period, the mentees became extremely stressed and started struggling emotionally, as they wanted the deal to go through as soon as possible.

This was their first deal, and I understood the emotion of wanting it to go through swiftly. This is a dangerous zone for most businessmen and women. Emotion can overtake rational thought and you can end up making very careless and costly decisions that can be detrimental to future projects.

On the day the contract was supposed to be signed, we could not reach our representative for twenty-four hours. This added more stress to an already stressful situation. My phone was constantly going off with messages from them. In my former mindset, I would allow their stress to affect me and impact my day, but I was able to compartmentalise that single issue and be patient in its resolution.

As I have evolved through my entrepreneurship journey, I have learned not to stress over things that I cannot control. There is always a solution to every problem. Eventually, the situation reached an amicable end with all parties satisfied. The brothers in reflection commented on how calm I remained throughout the process. I gave them the same lessons I am giving here. The two brothers now have altered mindsets and have started to see changes in areas of their lives.

I learnt this lesson quite early in my journey to become the man I am today. It was not a sudden epiphany, but a series of trial and error and I am still not there yet. There are occasions more frequently than I like that I regress into the old mindset and old habits. In these times I reach out to my spirituality or go away from the hustle and bustle to get my myself recanted and focussed.

3rd TIP *Take regular timeouts to recharge physically and mentally.*

Do not think the right mindset will appear overnight. That is an impossible task. You will fall back into old habits many times, unconsciously, but do not beat yourself up about it. We are all human beings and prone to making mistakes. If life was easy, then we would all be success stories. I spent years developing my current mindset after learning from my mistakes.

4th TIP Never walk away from a challenge or obstacle without learning the lesson, otherwise life may repeat the lesson until you get it.

A positive mindset starts with positive thinking. This may sound quite easy, but it is a challenge for most people. We are psychologically programmed to dwell on the negatives. It keeps us safe and it is a part of our survival mechanism that we are born with.

Let me elaborate briefly. Let us say you go on a walk in the forest and you choose the path to your left and you had a pleasant experience and you do it many times. The next time you go for a walk, choose the path to your right, and you will be attacked by a swarm of hornets nesting in a tree there. Which experience are you most likely to remember?

Are there hornet attacks? Correct. Why? Because your safety is threatened, and you recall the pain and do not want it repeated. You are in survival mode, so you may not go back to that forest ever again, even though the pleasant experiences greatly outweigh the one negative experience. Forgetting the negative puts, you at risk, whereas forgetting the positive has no real observable consequences.

It means developing a positive mindset involves overriding your default setting. We have to consciously tell ourselves to think positively until it becomes a habit. It is a slow process, but it will help you not only create a successful life but also give you the peace to enjoy it.

One of my mentors told me early in my property journey when I started moaning about how hard business was and crying out about the challenges, I was going through both in my business and personal life. Every time I would do that, he would tell me to endure because I was going through a period of growth. And he was right. Every challenge brought out a newer version of me and gave me a more open mindset.

Even 50 cents said 'Sunny days wouldn't be special, if it wasn't for rain. Joy wouldn't feel so good if it wasn't for pain'. I encourage you to obtain a positive mindset and keep on pushing through your challenges. There's a light at the end of the tunnel.

CHAPTER 5

THE VISION

"The most pathetic person in the world is someone who has sight but no vision."
— Helen Keller

Can you imagine driving down a one-way street at top speed with your eyes closed, hoping to get to your destination?

Scary, isn't it?

Yet so many of us make this decision, whether consciously or unconsciously, to live our lives in the same manner. Many people have been on autopilot for years and have made no attempt to regain control of their lives. They live in hope that somehow, one day, life will suddenly change, and everything will be as they dreamed it could be. This point of view is irrelevant to culture, geographical location, age, or intelligence; it is just a fact. Most human beings are lazy, and they are at their laziest when it comes to working on their own lives.

In fact, they invest more energy criticizing those who change the narrative than they invest in improving their own life. It is time to redirect that energy and work on yourself.

**4th CHALLENGE **

Create a vision statement for your life.

A vision statement is a document that states the current and future objectives. It is intended as a guide to help you make decisions that align with your ethos and pre-set goals. It is a roadmap to where you would like to be within a certain time-frame.

Remember this in creating your personal vision statement.

- Be concise.

- Be specific.

- Set a specific timeframe

- Set challenging goals.

Try to read other companies' vision statements as a template for your life.

The lifeline to your vision is to your imagination. There are no barrier limits and no barriers inside your imagination. Just ask any child before the world start building barriers of impossibilities and limits for them. Decades ago, driverless cars and mobile phones only existed in the imagination of people. What makes the seemingly impossible achievable is the action you take to get to the vision.

My journey towards being a property magnate started in the Democratic Republic of Congo about seventeen years ago. I grew up within an extended family network with my mother and maternal relatives as my father was living in Europe.

Life was relatively good; I can still remember the freedom and the games we played as children. One of my favourite games involved dreaming about our future. It was interesting that even though we had never experienced more than our current environment our imagination led us to places we have never been, and we had no idea how we were going to get there. I remember in numerous occasions I would go sleep early to consciously envision myself living in Europe.

My cousin Magloire shared the same dreams, and we would spend many hours carefully constructing the vision, adding more details as time elapsed. Our first dream at six years of age was to own a huge mansion with ten bedrooms and a swimming pool. Of course, growing up with boys was all about competition, and so my cousin would speak of his mansion, but it would have twelve bedrooms and two swimming pools. We would always try to out-do each other. On one occasion, we were sent to the market by our auntie to buy a few groceries in the borough of Matete, and on our way back I told him my mansion would have a petrol station and a runway for my private jet. Do not laugh too loud, John Travolta's mansion has its own runway for his private jet and Bryan Christopher Williams know by his stage name Birdman has its own petrol station in his mansion. Dreams can come true.

By the age of nine, I was becoming more aware of my daydreams. Going to school taught me about my limitations where before I had none. This in itself is an interesting concept, as schools are meant to educate you so that you can live the most fulfilling life possible. These limitations temporarily placed my dreams on hold. Teachers told me I was not smart enough for Set 1 and I could barely speak English, which limited my communication skills. The longer I attended school, the further my dreams drifted from becoming a reality. I am not advocating that schools are useless or dream killers, but I do believe our education systems need a drastic MOT to ensure it is fit for purpose. Children should be taught and encouraged to be creative and pursue their dreams and passions. Schools should equip them to make informed decisions and banish self-limiting philosophies that have become archaic and obsolete.

When I left school, I started to daydream once again, but this time I had actions behind my dreams, so they evolved into a plan. Simply stated, my vision is to create a legacy, not just for myself but to pave the way for other young men like myself. Whatever I visualize, I do so in great detail.

At the age of 28, I published two books called *The Rent-To-Rent Blueprint and The Rent-To-Rent Blueprint II.* That in itself was an accomplishment for me. You may think it was not that great, but remember that English was not my first language and throughout high school I struggled and was teased mercilessly about my accent and limited comprehension of the English language. Not only did I publish my first book, but it went on to become an Amazon Bestseller. Going forward, I intend to publish at least one book each year.

When I shared the news with my mother, she was very happy. She then told me that when I was

younger, I had confided in her that I would be some-
body one day. This comes back to the previous idea
of ensuring you bridge the gap between the mental idea and the real world. You can either write it
or speak it, but make sure it is in the real world, so
it becomes a tangible thing with real prospects of
becoming one. Proof that a vision can become a
reality.

We have a system in our bodies called the reticular activating system (RAS) that helps our brains
decide what information to focus on and what to
delete.

When you have a clearly defined purpose, a mis-
sion, and when you live every moment in a state of
certainty that you'll achieve it, you influence what
your RAS filters out and what lights it up. As a re-
sult, you pay special attention to things that help
you achieve what you're after, things you otherwise
would have never noticed.

CHAPTER 6

ACTION

A vision without action is merely a dream.
Action without vision just passes the time.
Vision with action can change the world
- James Christensen

Vision and action must go together to determine your success. They are partners with a shared destination. They exist symbiotically and are not mutually exclusive. As the CEO of your life, you need to set the vision and direct the actions that will take you from the virtual to the real.

I like to see the abbreviation GPS whenever I think about my life and strategizing my next move. Obviously, the abbreviation isn't new, but I have adopted and adapted it for my purpose. Once my vision is clear, I start setting my GPS for destination success. How do I accomplish this?

Allow me to share the method I used with you.

G stands for Goals.

Goals are not the vision. Goals are simply the steps you take in order to achieve a vision. For example, if your vision is to be a property investor, then your goals could be to create a million-pound portfolio or assemble a team that will help you achieve that goal. Goals are extremely important because they break down the process into manageable steps that provide the opportunity to reflect, refocus, and redirect your journey towards success.

I know most people are familiar with the **S**pecific **M**easurable **A**chievable **R**elevant **T**imed (S.M.A.R.T.) goals model. It has worked well for many others so let's not waste time reinventing the wheel. This is a good model to use when setting your goals. It helps you to focus your goal setting techniques and incorporates the specificity I mentioned earlier in Chapter two.

Follow the following steps in creating your vision.

• *Write down your vision with as much clarity as possible.* Try and include some specifics and aspects that may engage different senses. If your vision is on a mansion, what does the front door look like? Is it red or black? Is there a lavender aroma as you walk up because of the overgrown lavender bush at the entrance? Can you hear the neighbour's children laughing and splashing in the swimming pool next door? What time of year is it? Are you hot or is it raining?

Remember also that we visualise and dream in pictures, so focus on the pictures of your dream. If you really want to get to the next level, actually experiencing your vision before you get there is extremely powerful.

How can we do this? Visit open houses to see, feel and smell the type of house you want to live in. Test drive the car you would like to own one day. Everything becomes real once you have touched it.

The power of visualisation extends beyond your personal life. It is scientifically tested and employed by major business organisations and sporting teams who recognise its value for their success. Visualisation is one of the most used psychological skills by top athletes.

"Visualization, for me, doesn't take in all the senses," said Emily Cook, the veteran American aerialist. "You have to smell it. You have to hear it. You have to feel it, everything."

"The more an athlete can imagine and visualize the package, the better it's going to be," said Nicole Detling, a sports psychologist with the United States Olympic team. It is a multi-sensory experience that fast-tracks dreams and converts them into reality. These are experts in their fields who recognise and validate the importance of visualization.

Some people create vision boards so they can see the vision. Do not underestimate the power of this. Have you ever noticed that if you buy a yellow car or break your leg, then suddenly you start seeing more yellow cars and people with broken legs? The universe did not suddenly increase the number of yellow cars or broken legs. You're simply more focused on these things, so you start seeing them more often. This is known as reticular activation. When I purchased my Jaguar XF, all I saw on the road were Jaguar XF's. I never noticed them before I bought mine. From a distance, I could tell if it was an XF from the shape and sound. They were everywhere.

This is the same process that your brain goes through when you create a vision board. You will start seeing more opportunities or people that will help you on the way.

- *Display your vision in a place where you will see it daily. This is to keep it in your mind. Quite often, we set dreams and then push them to the back of the mind. In a twenty-four-hour cycle, most people may think about their actual vision about two or three times per day. This equates to less than 5% of your time. Like it or not, life gets in the way most of the time. In fact, we worry more than we think about our dreams. We daydream more than we think about our dreams. We all experience moments when we are thinking about absolutely nothing. What a waste of our precious minds!*

- If your dream is always in front of you, then it will be kept in the forefront of your memory and you will be less likely to forget it. It will register in the subconscious that it is possible.

I keep my vision board in my bedroom. It is the first thing I see when I open my eyes. I also keep a duplicate copy of my vision board in my car because I spend a lot of time driving around the country. That time can easily be wasted thinking about matters that are irrelevant and frivolous. As soon as my mind wanders off, I am confronted by my vision board, staring at me in the face. A reminder that I am going somewhere.

- *Identify all the prerequisites needed to accomplish your vision. Do* you need to gain some educational qualifications or skills? Do you need a license or certain experience? These are some of the questions you must answer at the start of your journey. Put the foundation in place before you start your journey. It makes no sense for you to turn up at the airport to travel the world and have no travel documents.

Do your research. This may seem time-consuming initially, but it will save you time in the long run. We have all heard the adage 'If you fail to plan, plan to fail'

I have always hustled and flipped anything I could get my hands on for a profit. After a while, I realised that the amount of effort invested did not equate to the profit I was earning. I then started thinking about a type of business I could invest my effort and time that would give huge rewards and be sustainable.

After careful and detailed research, it became apparent that property investments provided the life I was seeking and tied neatly into the goals I had set. Conversations with established business moguls revealed that most had an extensive real estate portfolio. Savvy rappers such as Young Jeezy, T.I, Master P and Jay Z always talk about owning land. I once watched a seminar by Dr Myles Munroe and he said, 'If you want to become wealthy, own land, and that is real estate.'

Years ago, I was on the train going home from my recruitment job when I happened to see an advert in the metro newspaper about becoming financially free by using property investment as a vehicle. It immediately captured my attention. It was as if the universe had seen my vision and was directing my path. Remember my story about the Jaguar XF?

I registered for the free seminar and at the end there was an offer for a three-day training course, which I purchased. At the time, I did not have the funds to invest in property. I decided I needed to investigate other options. To further my research, I started attending various property events, free seminars and joining different groups on Facebook. At one property networking event, I started talking to a gentleman and I expressed my vision and limitations. He then suggested a property strategy called rent to rent. If you have very limited finances, and want to get into property investment in the UK, renting to rent is one of the most successful strategies. It allows you to control someone else's property and make substantial cashflow from it.

If you would like to know how the strategy works, feel free to purchase a copy of 'The rent-to-rent Blueprint and The Rent-To-Rent Blueprint 2' from Amazon. To learn more about rent-to-rent I paid for a training session which lasted one day. As I was not getting the success I wanted, I contacted the trainer and asked him to mentor me privately. You must recognise the need to liaise and learn from people who are doing what you want to do. They can add tremendous value and their expertise is priceless in terms of developing your business acumen and starting you on your journey towards success.

- *Identify the steps needed to get to your goal. You can use time or the amount of money required to determine what constitutes each stage of the process.*

Some people classify these as short-term, medium-term or long-term goals, but I tend to use stages.

First Stage

Defining my final long-term goal this hardly changes. My long-term goal is financial independence and creating a financial vehicle I can pass onto my future generation. But remember I told you about specificity in goal creations? I have an exact figure in mind, but I choose not to share this yet!

Second Stage

Work backwards to create five things that must be in place before you can accomplish this goal. Reaching a goal must never be like rushing to build a home without the proper foundations in place. You may get there, but you won't stay there. One of my five things is to gain some education in financial investments and money management.

This stage was incorporated late into my journey. On my first trip towards financial freedom, I was just like that builder rushing to build his house without the proper foundation. I started spending recklessly and almost ruined my business.

You must stay focused on your goals and dreams, recognising each successful milestone but remaining cognizant that this is not the final destination. When I started seeing the first blooms of the work, I had put into my property investment, I forgot about the next milestones that I needed to reach to ascertain the financial freedom I sought.

Patrick Bet David once said on his Instagram account when talking about Connor McGregor's victory against Donald Cerrone. The moment you start making money, the following elements are heavily ignored: training, discipline, gratitude, reading, improvement, and blind spots. All these become your blind spots; when you weren't making money, you focused on those things to achieve success.' He could have been talking about my life.

When I started making money on rent to rent, I lost focus and my confidence in securing property deals was so high that I stopped making logical business decisions. A property strategy called serviced accommodation was born. Without educating myself on the model, I immediately jumped into it and lost a substantial amount of money because I lacked knowledge and discipline. I did not follow my own advice on doing detailed due diligence on properties I was taking on.

Third Stage

Check your circle. It sounds very simple, but it is an absolute requirement. You need to be aware of who surrounds you. Remember, sometimes when you break down and people run to help, you cannot see who is pushing or who is just pretending. Study your circle. In T. I's classic album Paper Trail, he has a song called "Collect Call." In the last verse of the song, he says, "When you're on top, everybody wants to ball with you, but when you're not, you wouldn't even know who to call, would you?" The key ingredient here is to keep everyone under scrutiny about who you choose to retain in your circle.

Your close relationships have the ability to influence your decisions and dictate your choices. It is not possible to avoid all human contact as human beings are sociable animals. It is, however, possible to choose who you want to surround you

Fourth Stage

It's about you. Mentally, physically, and emotionally, you have to be fit. I give my workout routine and relaxation time as much importance as pushing hard for success. Remember, you're trying to get somewhere, but you still need to enjoy the journey. As a certified fitness coach, I know the importance and benefits of being physically fit. It impacts your mental alertness, reaction time and focus. If you are not physically active, I suggest you start out slowly. A basic routine includes exercising at least 3 times per week for a minimum of 30 minutes.

Dreams can come true, but make sure you can enjoy success.

Fifth Stage

Reflect on and update your goals on a regular basis. The world and you are constantly changing. Change with it or risk getting left behind.

When I was growing up, Kodak and Woolworth were names that featured highly in any business success story. Where are they now? They fail to change and adapt, and the world leaves them behind.

- Be sure to always remember to celebrate each milestone you achieve, even the tiny ones. They are reminders that you're moving in the right direction.

- Continue learning; it never stops.

- Monitor your close network and never be afraid to walk away.

- Keep healthy and focussed.

"P stands for position!

Before you start your journey towards any preconceived destination you must assess your position relative to that goal. This will not only help you to save time and money, but it will also help you to focus thereby eliminating any wasted effort.

Assessing your starting position reduces repetition of things you have already accomplished and could potentially save you from many costly mistakes. Past successes and failures must be revisited to eliminate the potential of making the same mistakes twice.

When I first started on my property journey, I lacked adequate finances to fund any property deal. Even if you may have some funds; to propel your business to grow rapidly you need cash injection from investors. I identified this early in my journey and knowing where I was starting enabled me to make certain decisions quickly.

Armed with the knowledge of my starting position I planned my next steps. To attract investors, I started to use my social media as a stage to forecast what I was doing and sharing my journey. This helped to position me in front of people that wanted to get into property but did not have the time, so they leveraged my time, knowledge and experience while I leveraged their cash to secure deals.

S stands for START.

Answer this question. Five friends and I sat one day having lunch at a round table. If everyone sitting in an even number of positions decides to order a hamburger and the rest eat nothing, how many hamburgers were ordered?

I will leave you to think about this for a few minutes or weeks before I give you the answer.

There are millions of great ideas born every year that could change our world to a phenomenal degree. So why do we still have an energy crisis or cancer remains without a cure even though many ideas are being generated? It boils down to one main reason.

Most people do not begin working on their dream. Most of the time, we talk ourselves out of our own dreams by focusing on the challenges and difficulties ahead. But how else would we grow? The body builder does not wake up one morning and lift 100kg of weights, does he? He has to work through the pain and sweat. Then and only then will he know he is ready for competition.

CHAPTER 7

EXECUTIVE POSITIONS

"Efficiency is doing the thing right.
Effectiveness is doing the right thing."
- Peter Drucker

Every successful company assigns people to roles based on their expertise, skills, character-istics, and experience. People are employed in roles that suit their qualifications. I am sure no one would ever turn up to a solicitor's office to get treatment for a broken limb. As qualified as a lawyer may be, the fact is, he or she is not an expert in medicine. Asking a lawyer for medical advice would be silly, right?

Yet in our lives, we sometimes turn to people who have no experience, expertise, or qualifications for the problems we are facing, but we expect them to offer advice and solutions. Some people even get surprised when the advice does not work to their advantage.

"Be careful when a naked person offers you a shirt."
~ African proverb.

Although living your life like a CEO means you have to take on several roles, please do not assume you are an island and can do everything by your-self. We all need help sometimes and recognising when we do is a strength that is reserved for people with an open mindset. This is the very reason some people repeat self-sabotaging behaviours with-out any inclination that they can alter something in their lives to change the outcome.

In fact, society relies on these people for their systems to work. It is designed to capitalize on the masses who do not recognise that they are the CEO of their lives and instead opt to believe that other people determine their destiny.

I can safely estimate that ninety percent of the people who buy and read this book are not in their dream job. Many will complain every day about their boss, their jobs or their colleagues, but never alter one thing to change their lives. They will moan about the traffic, the clients, or the salary, but few will look beyond their current situation and change something to make it better. We are pre-programmed to be in the comfort zone with terms such as job-security, regular salary, and pensions. These ideas keep us stationary, and over time, we develop a fear of stepping outside our comfort zone or doing anything that would put us at risk.

Fortune favours the risk takers. Ask anyone who has had success. They will tell you the journey they travelled to be the CEO of their lives. They will share the challenges and triumphs they endured.

The CEO

The chief executive officer makes all the key decisions. If the decision needs the input of others, then the CEO selects the right people to provide the information or service. Many people think this is an easy job, but it is by far the most complex, energy-draining, and focussed. The greatest advantage is, of course, the positive outcomes. The CEO is the only person who needs to know something about everything. He or she makes the decision which could affect everyone.

Now most companies will have displayed in the front of their offices their vision statement and most will have the company's objectives for all to see. Employees will be given a copy of the company's ethos and their policies and procedures documents before they even start working. This is to make potential employees aware of the company's position on matters they deem important. These company documents outline the boundaries and the consequences associated with crossing these boundaries. In expectation of your adherence to these pre-established boundaries, you are asked to sign a contract. This contract will contain the terms and conditions of employment. Expected behaviours and a clear description of your role and compensation.

Although I am in no way encouraging you to do the same in your life, I would ask you to consider the advantages of outlining these early in any relationship you form in your professional and private life.

Human beings are communal animals and so we will interact with other human beings whether we choose to or not. Friends and friends of friends. Classmates and colleagues. Business associates and clients. The list is endless. But who determines the boundaries of these relationships? You? Or are you dragged along in whatever direction the relationship is headed?

I can tell you that very few people determine the boundaries of their relationships. People struggle with establishing boundaries even with inanimate objects such as food. When it comes to others, most people are afraid of upsetting the other parties and may even do or say things that they would not normally do because they want to 'fit in'.

When I embarked on my entrepreneurial journey, I had to terminate and distance myself from a few people who I regarded as friends and family. I had a close friend from school days that I shared everything with. Secrets, dreams, plans, hurt, joy, everything. We partied together. Wherever you saw me, you would see him. They called us *Buy One, Get One Free*. If you invited me somewhere, he would automatically show up and vice versa. We were a team.

Then my focus in life shifted. I wanted to become more, and I started chasing my dreams instead of chasing females, partying, spending frivolously. My priority had done a complete one hundred- and eighty-degrees direction change. Achieving my goals was my focus therefore, I had to distance myself from my dear friend. The activities we engaged in were no longer serving a purpose for me or helping me to achieve my vision.

I believed in investing for the long term; he believed in living for the moment and surviving from paycheck to paycheck. I believed in becoming an owner, but he wanted a regular salary and a position within someone else's company.

Time is our greatest asset and, unfortunately, not one we can recover. Once time is spent, it is spent. We have a limited time on this earth, so we need to choose how we spend it. I started to connect with the people that were on the same wavelength as me, so we could push and support each other. Though it was painful to distance myself, it served me well and, looking back, I have no regrets. I am glad I took charge of my fate and made that decision early.

As the CEO of your life, you need to tell people how to treat you and where the boundaries are. It may sound harsh, but it is not, and most of the time, setting the boundaries does not even involve saying a word. Sometimes just a look can be significant. For example, refusing to laugh at an offensive joke when everyone else is laughing sends subliminal messages to those present. If another offensive joke is shared within the same friendship group at another time, and once again you refuse to laugh, the chances of that reoccurring are slim. Without saying a word, you have essentially informed all present that you do not enjoy or find these jokes amusing. You have now established a boundary without speaking a word. The next time a similar joke comes up, they will be wary of saying it in your presence.

You can set your boundaries for relationships in many ways. We also do so by the clothes we wear, the places we go and the words we use. Constantly monitor these things.

EXECUTIVE POSITIONS | 75

'Your network determines your net worth'
~ Les Brown

Once you have erected the boundaries within your various groups, you need to be very strict about who you let behind those fences. It is much easier for those close to you to do more damage than your enemies. A hip-hop artist by the name of Plies once said, "the more you open yourself to someone, the more dangerous they become". Find people you can trust early in your journey and keep them close.

One of my most admired CEOs is Warren Buffet. He is from Nebraska, USA and the CEO of Berkshire Hathaway. He has a net worth in excess of US$80 billion. His alias is the 'Oracle of Omaha'. The most intriguing thing about Warren Buffet is his ability to stick to his decisions regardless of what is happening in the world. He made his millions investing in stocks, but most of his decisions went contrary to what was recommended by the majority. Warren Buffet was unique in many ways and was the CEO of his own life.

One of Warren Buffet's favourite quotes is *'You can only see who is not wearing trunks when the tides go out'*. This means that we may not always be able to see what those closest to us are doing until they are confronted with adversity, which reveals their true colors. He has lived this philosophy as the CEO of his own life.

Buffet remained married to the same woman for over ten years. Although that may seem normal, there is more to the story. His wife, Susan, actually left him to pursue her dream of being a singer, and he started a new relationship with Astrid Menks. The three remained in this unconventional arrangement because Buffet wanted to keep his boundaries tight. His friendship spans many decades.

The CEO is also responsible for accountability. He must stand by his decisions and be held accountable for the outcomes. Because of the potential implications, he or she must consider each decision before it is made.

To be the CEO of your life, you must pay greater attention to the choices you make and the likely consequences. It starts with simple decisions like, do I need to spend two hours scrolling through Facebook or is fifteen minutes sufficient? Do I call up a friend for a long chat or read a book? These simple decisions can have a far-reaching impact on your life. Spending an extra thirty minutes per day reading equates to over a hundred and eight hours per year. Enough time to make you an expert in a specific area or improve your life.

Once the decision is made, do you follow through to see how it affects your life? We need to think before we act because we should hold ourselves accountable for the life we lead.

If your life at this moment is not where you want it to be, stop right here and complete the challenge below.

5th CHALLENGE

Answer the following questions truthfully. Choose any day from the past week.

1. Can you account for all your waking hours?

2. Have you ever planned a day in its entirety?

3. Do you write down a list of daily tasks you need to accomplish?

4. How much time do you spend on social media?

5. Did you spend any time reading?

6. Have you learnt anything new recently?

Are you worth the investment of thirty minutes per day of your life? Then why aren't you doing it? Start now.

Accountant

Another integral role in the creation of a successful company and a successful life is accounting and accountability, which both complement each other. Money is an important aspect of living in the 21st century, yet few people have mastered the basic skills that are prerequisites for success. The bottom line is you need more money coming in than going out. There is no other way to accumulate wealth and the lifestyle you want.

So, let's do a simple exercise right now. Get a plain piece of paper and draw a line down the centre. Start by labeling one side income and the other expenditure, then start listing.

Before too long, you will realise that one column clearly exceeds the other by a few centimetres.

Now before I have the sceptics reminding me that there are people in this world with just one income and although they have several outgoings are still succeeding, I would have to ask them what percentage of the world's population falls in this category?' In fact, I would go further and ask, "How many people in their immediate circles fall into this category?"

The plain truth is the majority of us practise poor financial strategies to foster our growth and success. This book is especially targeted at these people. For any measure of success or to start your success journey, you must become financially aware of your incoming and outgoing and consciously work to establish a balance.

Here are some simple, manageable, and effective everyday techniques that can work without much disruption to your life. These will ease you into a changed mindset by helping you shift the way you think and change your current paradigm. Repeating this daily or weekly will slowly develop into established habits for life. Have you ever heard the adage, "Take care of the pennies and the pounds will take care of themselves"? Well, it means if you watch the small amounts of money you waste, the bigger savings will suddenly appear.

Here are just few tips. I've deliberately left two blank spaces for you at the back of the book to add two other things that may be an issue for you:

a. Make a list. Is that simple? Yes. A list does many things for you. It helps you manage your most important asset – your time. It provides accountability to your CEO so that minimal time is wasted.

b. A list also ensures you follow a prescribed path instead of wasting time, energy, and money elsewhere. When you go to the supermarket, go with a list. Check your cupboards before you leave so you know exactly what you need and only purchase what you need. Ignore the sale tags. I can guarantee you that sales are like buses; there will be another one in a few weeks. Remember, these stores need to sell! Sell! Sell! so sales are a part of their strategic forecasting. You will not miss out.

c. Regularly checking your bank statements weekly or monthly is recommended. Highlight purchases that could have been avoided. Re-mind yourself not to repeat that mistake next month.

    d. Set a target limit on those weekly expenses you can control, like food, petrol, clothing, etc., and stick to it.

    e. Create a monthly/weekly budget.

    f. Research passive income streams to generate additional income.

After adopting a few healthy habits, then it's time to be the accountant of your life. Create an accurate accounting system. You do not need any formal training to do this. Simply go back to the income and expenditure list you created and monitor the amount next to each entry.

I learnt this lesson the hard way. When I started my property journey, I knew I would be making money eventually and I couldn't wait to start spending. I knew I wanted to have money, but I had no firm plans as to how I would invest the money I earned.

Money, I have learnt, is not your friend. Think about it. It has no allegiance to anyone; it simply floats from one hand to the next without any problems.

When I saw the money growing in my bank account, I caught the spending bug and bought anything I wanted whenever I wanted it. I love to travel and have done it. I would spend thousands of pounds on travelling all over the world. I didn't even spend time checking for deals or discounts. I didn't need to because I could afford it. I had quite a few *'friends'* at that time and I treated them regularly. Not just your high street -names, but proper high-end brands. There was no limit. For the ladies I was dating, they had the time of their lives. I would take them into shops and ask them what they wanted and just let them choose. No limits. I spent like a king but acted like the joker.

I was bleeding cash from the business and making all the wrong choices. I had no other job, yet I hired a property manager. That freed up my time so I could waste my time. It did not take long until the inevitable happened. My business started haemorrhaging cash and I knew I was in trouble.

I realised I needed to assess my current circumstances and start doing some serious planning. Not only did I conduct a business audit but also a life audit.

I analysed my bank statement thoroughly and started getting rid of expenses that I did not need. I clearly did not need two vehicles and the cost of insurance was high considering my age and driving records. Rather than spending my money frivolously, I started to look for projects to invest in so that my money started working hard for me. I believe in giving and it will come back to me. Therefore, I started donating to charities that solve the causes that touched me deeply. By doing this practice, I significantly reduced my outgoings by thousands and increased my income.

My spending now is very strategic, and I strongly believe this model will help you significantly manage your income. Below is an early example of how I managed my income.

Firstly, I give myself a wage from my endeavours and what is left I reinvest into the business or invest in other people's projects.

From my wage, I split it into the following:

- 50% goes into necessities, which includes anything that I need to survive, such as rent, food, etc.

- 10% goes into giving, such as charitable work or helping someone that is in financial need.

- 10% goes into education. This allows me to keep investing in myself by buying books, paying for seminars, or having mentors.

- 10% goes into play. This allows me to spend money on anything I want without feeling guilty, because at the end of the day, I am the one working hard to make this money. This is how I sponsor my travels and treat myself.

- 10% goes into investments. In this pot, I want to create an opportunity for my money to work for me.

- 10% goes into saving for any unforeseen situations.

Your percentages do not have to be divided exactly as mine, but you can work towards it. I keep a close eye on any expenses that leave my account.

One of the chief functions of accountants is conducting audits. This involves an intense scrutiny of every penny. Accountability is key. Only in your life will the accountant and the CEO be the same individual, so self-discipline is essential. Roles and responsibilities must be clearly defined, and the requisite hat worn when relevant. Money is not your friend.

Marketing Executives

Who are you?

Would you believe there are lots of people who need to seriously think before they answer that question?

And for many, even when they give an answer, it will be wrong. The truth is, most people do not know who they are. It may seem like the silliest question, but it can be the most difficult to answer.

People will define who they are based on what they do by answering, I am a doctor, or I am a cashier. People will define themselves based on their relationships with others. I am Timmy's father or Jane's friend. People will define themselves according to their emotions at the time. I am a happy person. People will define themselves based on their biological gender. I am a woman or a man. People will define themselves based on their geographical location. I am Congolese, or I am American. These labels do not really say much about you. Who are you and what makes you unique? Isn't it amazing that even though there are billions of people on this planet, you are unique? No other version exists. You are the only copy. With this in mind, think about what defines you.

Be YOU! Everyone else is taken
~ Oscar Wilde

** 6th CHALLENGE **

Take some time and write down some things that make you unique! This is not a five-minute task. It may take you quite a while to get to know yourself and identify things that make you unique. Some people never find the true answer to this question.

If you are struggling to define who you are, imagine the difficulties others may be facing in defining who you are. You may find that who you are changes over time with new experiences. The blueprint, however, will always be the same. Your core values and beliefs should be your template.

To start the journey of self-discovery, you first need to understand your past and accept your present. Your past is the blueprint for who you are now. All your experiences have helped to shape the individual you have become. Understanding your past helps you to determine what choices were successful and which ones had a negative impact on your current stage of your journey.

Armed with this knowledge, you can now accept where you are and focus more on the choices you now need to make going forward in your life. Once you know who you are and have a true understanding of why you are, then you can choose how to market yourself. Never try to typecast yourself into a role that is not transferable. What do I mean by this?

Everyone watches or has seen the television series Friends. Ross is a known goofy scientist in the series. When the series ended, he tried to make it in the movies, but the image of Ross became so embedded in everyone's mind that they just saw Ross in a different environment, never the new character. He is forever typecast as Ross.

In real life, this can happen with simple choices like tattoos, hanging out with certain friends or getting a criminal record. You may want to move on but are unable to do so due to the image you are associated with. Ensure that the image you create is one that synchronizes with your dream and represents who you are. Like it or not, we all judge people by their appearance, the way they speak and their past.

Social media platforms have become the marketing and advertising tools for personal brands. This has its advantages and disadvantages.

The advantages

- You can reach a much wider audience.

- You can monetise it

- You can create a platform to give value.

The disadvantages

- Everything you place on your platform is forever accessible, even after deletion.

- There could be trolls.

- Not everything is what it seems to be.

Always be careful of what you choose to post online. Think long term. Think of your vision. Think about your dream.

The importance of this is even more relevant in light of ongoing scandals involving very powerful people where their personal brand has been forever tarnished because of a simple photograph that has resurfaced. What may seem like a fun night out can be detrimental to your future. One simple bad choice can destroy your entire future.

Imagine being caught on camera every day. Science fiction or not? No, you do not need to imagine this because this is the reality of living in today's society. We are constantly being videotaped, so choose wisely.

I use social media differently than most people. Social media is a platform where I can help anyone who wants to take control of their own destiny by utilising quick educational videos and posts. I am very rough and raw with my brand. What you see is what you get. I am not your formal business guy with suite and tie, even though there's nothing wrong with this mode of dress, it is just not part of my brand.

Authenticity is key for me, so I display to people the *'real'* reality of my industry in comparison to other people in the same industry who make things look very easy, so everyone thinks they can do it without money or time. Anyone can do it, but they need the right mindset and education.

The majority of my mentoring clients have come from social media. They saw what I was doing and wanted to do the same, so they contacted and ended up becoming clients. I offer a much higher interest rate to my investors than normal banks would, so it makes financial sense for them to invest with me. However, the majority of these investors have come from social media, observing what I was doing and the opportunity I was offering, and they took advantage of it. Feel free to follow me on Instagram @napabafikele.

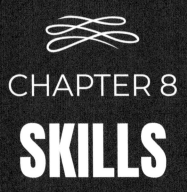

CHAPTER 8

SKILLS

You must always live a life of self-consciousness.
- Sunday Adelaja

The mindset helps us to focus on the vision and be in synchronicity with the universe. However, awareness does not substitute for the skills required to utilize what you now know and how to use it to your advantage.

The list below is by no means exhaustive, but I feel they are certain basic skills that must be cultivated, developed and used frequently. They are paramount to any success you may have, whether in your personal or professional life.

Listening is skill number one.

Such a simple skill, but it is rarely used, even when it has the potential to cause significant harm to your well-being. Be honest, after numerous research and scientific medical advice about the types and amount of food we consume, have you listened and adapted your lifestyle to reflect the knowledge gained?

Have you ever lost your temper after a few words and even before the person completes their statement? Have you ever seen something and got angry without hearing the reason or explanation behind the reaction?

We have become a reactive society with an impatience to listen carefully. It is estimated that most people will switch off videos if their interest is not engaged after ten seconds. Ten seconds, that is where our attention span lies.

'When we speak, we say only what we already know; but when we listen, we learn new things.'
~ Dalai Lama

My business partner once told me that you have two ears and one mouth. Use them in that ratio! That was a simple but valuable lesson for me. It made me pay closer attention when someone is speaking. I listened closely to his advice and was able to create a minimum of five different streams of income. I took that advice on board and made it a reality. Life is less stressful when you have various streams of income.

However, I am not perfect and there have also been times when I did not listen, and I suffered the consequences. My mother tells me constantly that I work too hard without resting and recharging. I will be on my laptop working for hours, and the moment I turn off my laptop, I will go onto my phone and work. It eventually started to affect my relationships with people around me, as I was not devoting time to them. I realised before it was too late and amended my work schedule. It's important to be observant and listen thoroughly to what is being said to you in all areas of your life. Hear something too many times? Don't ignore it.

In a poem called "The Industry" by DMX, there were a few lines that stood out to me and relate very much to this topic. I paraphrased due to the explicit language. "Often, my words fall on deaf ears. People are listening but don't hear. They'll be sitting right here if you talk to them. I was like, "Where are you going?!? "; he was like, "yeah". It shows that people are hearing but not listening to you.

Here are five tips that will turn you into a better listener:

1. Maintaining eye contact demonstrates to the speaker that you are paying complete attention to the interaction and are attentive and caring about it. Avoid wandering your eyes while texting, reading, writing, or watching television.

2. Avoid interrupting – this is critical because you want to give your speaker time to finish their point. If you want to interject or ask for more clarity, wait for a pause from the speaker prior to doing so.

3. Be prepared to listen – come into the conversation ready to receive the information objectively. Clear your mind from any disrupting thoughts and engage with the speaker during your conversation.

4. Practice mirroring – you want to mirror the speaker to demonstrate that you are paying attention to the conversation. Reflect the same energy or cues the speaker is giving to you back to them. If the speaker smiles, you want to smile back. Nod when you are seeking clues that you understand what they're saying to you.

5. Give positive non-verbal feedback–Be mindful of your body language. Your facial expression gives a clear indication of your thoughts and mood. Look at the person talking, point your body in their direction, and listen intently.

Social Awareness is skill number two.

People connect with individuals who they like. Are you likeable? No man or woman is an island so we must coexist in a shared space. It is imperative that we know our value, but we must also be aware of the value others bring and recognise it.

As the world of social psychology is fluid you must update your knowledge regularly to avoid any faux pas or cause offense to anyone. There are gender changes, new sexualities and a major shift in food choices and environmental consciousness. If you are to develop this skill you must engage in regular social activities. I am not advocating that you party daily, but you need to explore different settings to gain an open mind of all the possibilities and adapt your behaviour to create bonds and establish strong social connections.

Communication is skill number three.

Surveys conducted worldwide list lack of effective communication as the main reason relationships break down.

To communicate effectively you must first understand that communication is made up of three distinct components. The communicator must first research the best method of communication then send the message in a format or mode easily understood. The second component involves the receiver receiving and interpreting the message. The final stage is the receiver indicating that the message was received by providing a response to close the communication loop.

From the preceding paragraph you can clearly know how many things can potentially go wrong. Quite often, the method and mode of communication used are based on our personal choice, competency, or comfort. Little or no regard is given to the intended receiver. Have you ever been on holiday and seen an English person desperately shouting and gesticulating in English to a person who speaks a completely different language with the expectation that they will receive the message and give a positive response? It happens daily.

With the advent of text speaking, communication is now very restricted by a simple thing like age. Older folks have a completely different meaning for lol!

Another potential problem is when we send a message and assume the receiver gets it without checking. It is always wise to check what message was received.

Responding is skill number four.

It may seem irrelevant but learning to respond is an important skill in life. Your response to situations can have lasting effects on your life and help shape the path you take.

> *They may forget what you said — but they will never forget how you made them feel.*
> **—Carl W. Buehner**

When you respond, be mindful of the emotions attached to your response. A word uttered angrily can impact the receiver and bear heavily or negatively on future encounters. Always think before you speak. Remember, the bible reminded us that a soft answer turned away wrath. Never speak in anger. Take time to calm yourself before speaking.

Another often neglected area is body language. This is more difficult to control than actual words yet never get a lot of attention. Most pokers players wear shades to shield their eyes for one main reason. The eyes don't lie. In Eastern traditions people look in the eye for a sign of happiness and do not use the smile as an indicator, however, in the streets looking at someone in the eyes or as the street calls it, screwing someone can be a form of disrespect. Practise self-control and learn how to use your body to complement your words instead of detracting.

Awareness is also good because now you can also focus on people's eyes when you communicate to get their true emotions or feelings.

7th CHALLENGE

Stop for a few minutes and select one area of your life, personal, professional, or even spiritual. Think of a specific scenario and your response. My favourite is to focus on your immediate reactions when someone cuts you off in traffic. What is your first thought?

Furiously try to get back in front of them? Recklessly driving, so you can tell him exactly how you feel. Or just let it go?

How can you change one tiny thing to improve your reaction? Maybe try to understand their situation to rationalise it. For example, I was running late to work and had to attend an emergency, so the action was not conducted under malice intention. To calm yourself down, try some breathing exercises. Changing yourself is difficult, but if you make any improvements, you will gradually begin to see big results.

CHAPTER 9

MENTORSHIP

"If I have seen further, it is by standing on the shoulders of giants."
— Isaac Newton

n Chapter four on mindset, we spoke about being present in the moment and noticing the small, obvious details often missed by most people. Well, if you have been following my challenges and tips, here is your first test.

What is the inscription on the side of a two-pound coin? Most people have never really stopped to read it, but it is one of the most inspiring quotations. No, I am not going to tell you. The whole purpose of this book is not to spoon-feed you information but to challenge you to recognise your value and motivate you to get moving. Do you suppose the CEOs of Fortune 500 companies sit around waiting to be given information? No, they get up and go searching for it. So now you can go find out for yourself.

Nothing is wrong with being a trendsetter and creating paths where none existed before, but equally as important is not reinventing the wheel. Whether we make the decision consciously or subconsciously, we will all follow someone, somewhere, at some time in our life.

On May 6, 1954, Britain's Roger Bannister's name was written in the history books as the first person to break the 4-minute mile in Oxford, England. Up until that moment, scientists, sports enthusiasts and athletes believed this was an impossible feat. But how did Roger accomplish this seemingly impossible feat? He first created the vision in his head. It had to be inside his head because no one had ever done this before; there were no records or examples. He had to mentally create the scenario. In an interview, Roger told journalists that he relentlessly visualized the achievement in order to create a sense of certainty in his mind and body.

Once he had the picture, he relied on mentors and accepted the help of others who knew more about certain elements of his goal. Special shoes were made by a cobbler in London. His shoes were 50% lighter than his previous pair.

Roger also enlisted the help of the mountaineer Edmund Hillary, who gave him advice to help him develop his techniques. A few years later, that mountaineer used his routine to scale the highest mountain in the world, Mount Everest. They became mentors for each other, and this propelled them to success. Roger Bannister not only recognised the importance of creating a mental picture, but he was smart enough to enlist mentors who were knowledgeable in their field.

You will never know everything about anything.

I don't need to know everything; I just need to know where to find it when I need it'
~ Einstein

Every successful person has benefitted from a coach or mentor in their journey to success. You are no different. Having a mentor stretches and challenges you to push you out of your comfort zone. A great mentor should hold you accountable for your actions. They also help you to see the things that may be in your blind spot. They know the mistakes you're likely to make and can help you to avoid those pitfalls that can demotivate and prevent you from becoming the CEO of your life.

Most companies will occasionally invite in auditors or outside help to assess their effectiveness on a regular basis. They do this to ensure they remain on track, remain relevant and committed to their vision. Distractions happen in life and quite often we do not realise we are being distracted until it is too late. A mentor will be able to see more objectively and get you back on track sooner.

When I first became a property investor, I got demotivated because I had no experience in this field. The language was foreign to me and I struggled to make a success out of it. Even though I had taken a course specifically on rent-to-rent, I came across challenges and obstacles I did not have an answer for. Most importantly, I did not have anyone to turn to.

Some may say you do not need mentors because all the information today is online, but the first problem you will encounter is that '*everyone online tends to be an expert'*. You do not know whether the information you are getting will serve you well. Therefore, it is crucial for you to do your due diligence on the person you are following. You want to ensure the content creator does have practical experience with the subject matter.

What will you search for if you do not know what you are looking for? Even though I was trained before starting my Rent-to-Rent investment, landlords and agents asked me questions that I was not prepared for. I did not know how to handle it. I then decided it was time for me to get a mentor. I contacted the person who trained me and used my credit card to pay for his mentorship program. Though the payment approach was risky, the dividend I gained throughout my journey was worth it. That led immediately to my confidence being boosted. I had new knowledge, information and wisdom. I also had a sense of direction and accountability. If I came across an obstacle, all I had to do was contact him and he would guide me accordingly. I had an objective pair of eyes looking out for me.

Shortly after, my results started showing. Many years later, I commenced mentoring people on the same property strategy. When I analyse the results of the people I trained without mentoring and the people I trained with mentoring, you can see a significant difference. People who I trained and mentored tend to secure property deals faster, tend to run the business more successfully and their scalability is also greater than people without mentoring.

Choosing a mentor can be daunting. This must be done after you set your GPS. This will identify where your strengths and weaknesses are and help you to choose a mentor that will improve your weaknesses and sustain your areas of strength.

The bigger questions lie in the way you find a mentor. I worked with myriad mentors, coaches, and consultants, and a funny fact is that I noticed many offered advice based on their reading rather than experience. I found it fascinating how that industry functions when it comes to mentors. Patrick Bet David wrote a book called Your Next Five Moves and he covered three different levels you can choose a mentor: Theory, Witness, and Application.

Theory: mentors at this level may not be wise, but they are smart and tend to have degrees from prestigious universities. Many professors and consultants fall into this category. Wisdom is practical experience, and advice from these mentors gravitates toward a theory-based approach. They can tell you how to do something, but if you ask them if they have ever done it, the answer would likely be no. There are theory-based mentors, and there's nothing wrong with that. A property strategy is called a lease option. I read a lot about it and even had a one-to-one mentor to teach me the strategy, but I never actually did it. Therefore, I have knowledge of the strategy but no wisdom. They can still give good advice, but they're lower-level mentors.

These people have witnessed entrepreneurs building successful businesses, either by working with them directly or just being present in their environment. For example, Gomer Lukisa and Milvia Serra who has never done property business but has been around me pretty much every day, especially when conducting business. Their advice could be valuable as a mentor as their witnessed me at work. At a networking event, I was really impressed with how both was explaining to someone who wanted to know what a flying freehold was. To my surprise, I did not expect them to know. However, hearing me discussing the pros and cons with my students, Gomer and Milvia were able to pick it up and transcend that knowledge to others.

Application: Mentors from this category advise you with information coming directly from the source. These are the most valuable mentors as they tell you what they've done and what worked for them. It's crucial to learn from people that walk their talk. These mentors can share what worked for them and what did not. While doing rent to rent, I acknowledged the method I was taught on how to speak with an agent was no longer effective. I developed a new method that proved to be more effective and increased the success rate. I then taught those clients who were having difficulties passing through the agent gatekeepers my new improved method that enhanced their ability to get more viewings and have more offers accepted.

Mentors can be chosen from these three hierarchies, and all can provide immense value. However, it is important to do some due diligence to identify where the mentor sits in the categories. I believe a mentor from the application category is better equipped, especially if you are going through difficult times within your business.

Everything I do in life, whether it is personal or business, I always try to find someone that has done it successfully and get them to guide me. I had a mentor/therapist, when I had problems in my relationship. Most people tend to turn to friends and family for advice. They often turn to people who were also emotionally broken. I made a conscious decision that whoever I am dating, and we are going through our rough patches that we would not tell people our problems but find a professional and work with them. Working with my mentor in this area helped me to view things differently, it helped me to take my partner's emotion and feelings into consideration.

Public speaking is something I love doing. I am attracted to the idea of going on stage to help and inspire people to better their situations. As my property journey progresses, several organizations have begun to invite me to speak at their events. I then came to the realisation that public speaking is a skill that needs nurturing. There are so many elements that go into making your speech effective. For example, when you are speaking, the tone of your voice, your body language, and eye contact are all key to maximizing engagement and getting your message across. There are so many things to consider and I was unaware of this. I then decided to get a mentor in this field to help me improve my speaking skills and confidence.

In addition, mentors are only there to guide you, but the work must come from you.

CHAPTER 10

REFLECTIONS

"Sometimes, you have to look back in order to understand the things that lie ahead."
- Yvonne Woon

On more than a few occasions, I have heard or read quotes telling us that we must never look back and always look forward. I am going to rebel against the status quo and tell you that it is imperative that we look back in order to move forward. Looking back does not mean going back to where you were, but recognising how far you have come and all that you have overcome. Just a gentle reminder that you have survived can be the most uplifting emotion you ever experience. Looking back also gives you the foundation for gratitude and helps you to remain humble when you feel as if you have 'arrived' or tempted to feel as if you are above someone else.

This is a practice I regularly employ in my daily life. I am so grateful that my present life enables me to comfortably put a roof over my head and provide food on the table. I am now settled in my mind knowing that my daughter and all other future offspring will be financially secure and have no worries when it comes to their finances.

But I was not always at this point. More than five years ago, I found myself homeless, jobless, and hopeless. At age twenty-three, I was living with my parents and sister in London and was comfortable. As fate would have it, I walked in one day on a domestic situation and my protective instincts for my mother kicked in before I had time to process the possible consequences of my actions or reactions.

This book has honestly been a labour of love and an opportunity for me to share my personal journey and the lessons I have learnt along the way. I decided to write and share my story in the hope that it will inspire and motivate others to become more aware of who they are and to live the life they desire. The information and advice given is not exhaustive and not the complete guide to becoming the CEO of your life. Life is a journey and the process of learning, developing, and changing happens every day, whether it is planned or unplanned. Writing this book gives the blueprint of my journey.

If you have read up until this point, then I hope you have learnt at least one strategy or taken one piece of advice that you can implement in your life to effect the change you are searching for.

I believe every human being is born with an innate hunger to become more, but few rise to the challenges or persevere to overcome the obstacles to triumph. Every person who reads this book will identify with an idea or a thought presented here. Our journeys may be different, but we share similar experiences throughout our lives.

Remember to breathe and go at your own pace when discovering who you are. This is not an overnight change; it will require many days or even years, but the effort invested will be worth it.

FINAL CHALLENGE

Before you finish this book and store in on your bookshelf for the next few years, set your GPS and go.

CONTACT

Facebook: Napa G Bafikele

Instagram: Napa Bafikele

LinkedIn: Napa Bafikele

YouTube: Napa Bafikele.

Make sure you subscribe to my YouTube channel for regular free content.

To find out about my training and mentoring packages, please visit www.napabafikele.com

Notes:

Printed in Great Britain
by Amazon